Crafts From Your Favorite Fairy Tales

By Kathy Ross
Illustrated by Vicky Enright

The Millbrook Press
Brookfield, Connecticut

For my sister Bootsie,
my old partner in make-believe.
K.R.

For my fairy tale come true,
my husband, Tim.
And for Finny and Jake.
V.E.

Library of Congress Cataloging-in-Publication Data
Ross, Kathy (Katharine Reynolds), 1948-
Crafts from your favorite fairy tales / Kathy Ross ;
illustrated by Vicky Enright.
p. cm.
Summary: Provides directions for making puppets, mobiles,
puzzles, and more, featuring characters from twenty different fairy tales.
ISBN 0-7613-0259-X (lib. bdg.)   ISBN 0-7613-0342-1 (pbk.)
1. Handicraft—Juvenile literature. 2. Fairy tales in art—Juvenile literature.
[1. Handicraft. 2. Fairy tales in art.] I. Enright, Vicky, ill. II. Title.
TT160.R714228   1997
745.5—dc21   96-48517   CIP   AC

Published by The Millbrook Press, Inc.
2 Old New Milford Road, Brookfield, Connecticut 06804

Contents

Introduction

This is a book of crafts that features characters from twenty of the most widely read fairy tales. Some of the crafts, such as the puppets, will help you tell the story. Others are decorative objects that are based on a tale.

The fairy tales themselves are not included in the book. If you come across a project for a tale you are not familiar with, I hope you will be tempted to find that story. These fairy tales are available in many different versions, and all of them are here because I remember loving them when I was young! If your own favorite tale isn't here, you can do a craft anyway. Try making the "Story Box Theater" from *Rumpelstiltskin* or the "Box Puzzle" from *Puss in Boots* using any tale you like.

I hope these craft projects will make it even more fun to read and reread your favorite tales.

Kathy Ross

In the story **The Little Mermaid** the mermaid longs to replace her tail with legs so that she may live with the human prince.

Mermaid Mobile

Here is what you need:

9-inch (23-cm) heavy paper plate

blue plastic wrap

four cardboard toilet-tissue tubes

orange, pink, black, and red construction paper scraps

markers

blue yarn

string

green curling ribbon

gray poster paint and paintbrush

masking tape

12-inch (30-cm) blue pipe cleaner

scissors

white glue

hole punch

Here is what you do:

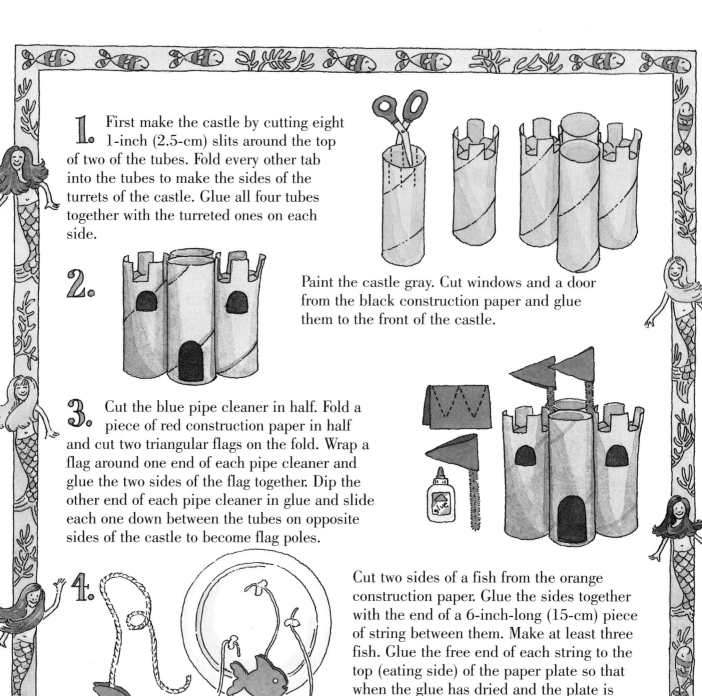

1. First make the castle by cutting eight 1-inch (2.5-cm) slits around the top of two of the tubes. Fold every other tab into the tubes to make the sides of the turrets of the castle. Glue all four tubes together with the turreted ones on each side.

2. Paint the castle gray. Cut windows and a door from the black construction paper and glue them to the front of the castle.

3. Cut the blue pipe cleaner in half. Fold a piece of red construction paper in half and cut two triangular flags on the fold. Wrap a flag around one end of each pipe cleaner and glue the two sides of the flag together. Dip the other end of each pipe cleaner in glue and slide each one down between the tubes on opposite sides of the castle to become flag poles.

4. Cut two sides of a fish from the orange construction paper. Glue the sides together with the end of a 6-inch-long (15-cm) piece of string between them. Make at least three fish. Glue the free end of each string to the top (eating side) of the paper plate so that when the glue has dried and the plate is turned upside down, the fish will hang from the plate.

5. Cut four 18-inch-long (46-cm) pieces of green ribbon. Curl each piece of ribbon. Glue one end of each ribbon to the top of the plate, among the fish, to look like seaweed hanging down. Let the glue dry before continuing.

6. Tear off two 18-inch-long (46-cm) pieces of blue plastic wrap. Hang one over the bottom of the plate with the ends hanging over the two sides of the plate. Hang the second piece across the first piece with the ends hanging down. This is the ocean water.

7. Punch four holes, evenly spaced, around the sides of the plate and through the plastic wrap. Cut four 12-inch-long (30-cm) pieces of blue yarn. Tie one end of each piece through a hole in the plate. This will hold the plastic wrap in place and become the hanger for the mobile.

8. Glue the castle off to one side on the plastic-covered plate bottom. Cover the area with masking tape first to create a better sticking surface for the castle.

9. Draw a mermaid on pink construction paper. Color the mermaid with markers and cut the picture out. Color the other side of the picture to look like the back of the mermaid. Cut a small slit in the plate. Slip the mermaid through the slit so that her tail is under the plate with the fish, as if she is underwater with her head above the water looking at the castle.

10. Tie the four ends of yarn together over the castle and the water to form a hanger for the mobile.

Hang the mobile at eye level so everyone can see above and below the water.

In **Snow White** and **Rose Red**, the beautiful sisters make friends with a talking bear. Do you know who the bear turns out to be?

Talking Bear

Here is what you need:

brown construction paper

pencil

black marker

Styrofoam tray

white glue

scissors

pinking shears

clamp clothespin

Here is what you do:

1. On brown construction paper, sketch a simple outline of a bear standing sideways.

Add details with a black marker, but do not draw a mouth. Cut the bear out.

2.

Use pinking shears to cut a 1-inch-long (2.5-cm) mouth for the bear. If you don't have pinking shears, try to cut a zigzag opening with regular scissors.

3. Rub glue along one side of the top and bottom clamps of the clothespin. Glue the top of the bear's mouth to the top clamp and its bottom jaw to the bottom clamp. Break off some pieces of Styrofoam to put between the clamps of the clothespin while the glue is drying. This will keep the two sides of the clothespin from gluing together.

When the glue has dried, the bear will be ready to talk. Just squeeze the end of the clothespin gently to open and shut the bear's mouth.

In the story **Rapunzel,** a wicked witch keeps a young girl in a tower that can only be entered by climbing up her beautiful golden hair.

"Rapunzel in Her Tower" Puppet

Here is what you need:

cardboard wrapping paper tube at least 2 feet (61 cm) long and 2 inches (5 m) wide

black poster paint and a paintbrush

pink construction paper

yellow and black yarn

newspaper to work on

white glue

markers

scissors

Here is what you do:

1. Cut eight 1½-inch (4-cm) slits around one end of the tube to make eight tabs. Fold every other tab down to make the top of the tower.

2. Cut out a 3-inch-square (8-cm) window near the top of the tower.

3. Paint the tower black and let it dry.

4. Cut a circle face out of the pink construction paper to fit in the tower window. Use markers to draw the facial features of a pretty girl on the pink circle. Glue bits of yellow yarn around the face for hair. Glue the face to one side and the bottom edge of the tower window.

this long

5. Cut ten strands of yellow yarn about three times as long as the height of the tower. Fold the strands in half and knot the folded end. Braid the yarn until you have a braid that is slightly longer than the height of the tower from the bottom of the tower to the bottom edge of the window. Tie a piece of yarn around the end of the braid to hold it in place. Trim off any extra yarn at the end of the braid so that there is only about 1 inch (2.5 cm) of fringe below the tie.

6. Cut a piece of black yarn the same length as the braid. Tie one end through the top loop of the folded-over yarn of the braid. Drop the other end through the window of the tower so that it falls out the bottom of the tower. Tie that end to the bottom of the braid.

7. To work the puppet, slide the braid up inside the tower window so that it is hidden. Say, "Rapunzel, Rapunzel, let down your hair, so that I may climb your golden stair." Pull on the black yarn coming out of the window so that the braid appears and comes all the way down to the bottom of the tower.

13

In Snow White and the Seven Dwarfs

Snow White thought at first that the cottage filled with small furniture belonged to children.

Seven Sleepy Dwarfs

Here is what you need:

two cardboard egg cartons

corrugated box cardboard

pink and blue poster paint and a paintbrush

14 wiggle eyes

fabric scraps in seven different patterns

7 small red pompoms

red construction paper

red rickrack

fiberfill

scissors

white glue

newspaper to work on

Here is what you do:

1. Cut a two-section piece out of one of the egg cartons. Cut the top off the second egg carton. Turn the carton over to form the head and body of six dwarfs lying down.

glue & tape →

Glue the section cut from the other egg carton to one end to make seven dwarfs in a row. Paint all seven egg-cup dwarfs pink.

2. Cut a headboard and footboard for the bed just slightly longer than the row of dwarfs. The headboard should be about twice as tall as the footboard. Paint the bed parts blue on both sides and let them dry.

3. Cut a square of fabric for a blanket for each dwarf. Glue a blanket around the bottom egg cup of each dwarf.

4. Glue two wiggle eyes and a pompom nose on each top egg cup to make a face for each dwarf. Rub glue around each face and glue on a fiberfill beard and hair.

5. Glue the headboard across the top of the dwarfs and the footboard along the bottom. You might want to put the bed between two heavy objects, like books, to hold the pieces in place while the glue dries.

6. Cut a heart for each dwarf from red paper, and glue it on the headboard over each head. Glue a strip of rickrack across the footboard.

These seven dwarfs are all tucked in and ready for a good night's sleep after a day of hard work. "Good night."

The **Princess** and the **Pea** tells the story of the search for a true princess, the only one sensitive enough to feel a tiny pea through piles of mattresses and blankets.

Stapler Blankets

Here is what you need:

- scissors
- fabric
- yarn or thin ribbon
- fiberfill
- stapler and staples
- permanent markers
- white glue

Here is what you do:

1. Fold the fabric in half and cut out a piece of fabric in the size you would like the blanket to be. Remember, if you make it too large, you will not be able to get the stapler to the center of the blanket to "stitch" it.

2. Spread a thin layer of fiberfill between the folded fabric. Staple around the fabric at 1/2-inch (1.5-cm) intervals to "stitch" the blanket to hold the fiberfill in place. Staple a pattern of stitches across the blanket in both directions to give it a quiltlike appearance.

3.

If you have used a solid-color fabric, you can draw a picture in each square of the blanket, using permanent markers.

4. If you have used a patterned fabric, you can glue on knotted pieces of yarn or ribbon to accent the staple "stitches."

Make a pile of blankets for your doll friends. Stack them up with a dried pea underneath to see if you have a princess.

...once up[on] a time [there] was a real[ly] neat big b[ear] and she re[ad]

...and they got married and lived happy... The end!

Thumbelina tells the story of a girl so tiny that she could sit in a flower.

Thumbelina in a Flower Glove Puppet

Here is what you need:

knit glove

piece of lace

felt scraps in several bright colors

yellow yarn

cotton swab

white glue

markers

scissors

Here is what you do:

1. Cut ten 3-inch (8-cm) flowers from felt of different colors. Cut a slit in the center of each flower so that it just slips over your finger. Slide two different color flowers about halfway down each finger of the glove.

10 –

2. Use the markers to draw a tiny face on one end of the stick that's left after cutting the cotton end off the swab. Unravel bits of yellow yarn and glue them around the face for hair.

3. Dip the opposite end of the swab in glue and tuck it down between one of the flowers and the finger of the glove. Dress the tiny girl by gluing on a piece of lace.

People will have to look very closely to discover which of the flowers in your garden is home for tiny Thumbelina.

Puss in Boots tells the story of a poor young man who receives a fortune through the cleverness of his cat.

Box Puzzle

Here is what you need:

nine small pudding or gelatin boxes of equal size

scissors

masking tape

white or colored paper

markers or crayons

white glue

Here is what you do:

1. Use masking tape to tape all of the boxes shut. Put strips of masking tape over the front of each of the boxes to create a better gluing surface.

2. On a sheet of paper, line up three rows of three pudding boxes, pushing them as close together as possible. Trace around the boxes on the paper. Trim the paper to exactly fit the boxes.

3. Draw your favorite picture from the story on the white paper.

4. Glue the paper to the nine boxes and let the glue dry.

5. Carefully cut the boxes apart to make a puzzle.

Mix up the box pieces of your picture and see if you can put it back together again.

In **Cinderella**, a young girl goes from rags to riches when she wins the heart of a handsome prince.

Rags to Riches Cinderella

Here is what you need:

light-colored poster board

scissors

fabric scraps for a work dress and a ball gown

white glue

stapler and staples

pretty trim for the ball gown

markers or crayons

Here is what you do:

1. Draw Cinderella from the waist up as she looked when she was a servant for her wicked stepmother and stepsisters. Use half of the poster board or less. Turn the picture upside down and draw another Cinderella with the waist starting at the end of the first picture. Draw this Cinderella with the top of a beautiful ball gown and her hair all done up for a party.

2. Cut two identical circles from the fabrics as wide as the height of both Cinderella halves. Make one circle out of dull fabric for her work dress. Make the other circle out of fancy fabric for the ball gown. Cut a slit in the center of each circle as wide as the waist at the center of the two dolls.

3. With the dull fabric circle on top and facing up and the fancy fabric on the bottom and facing down, slip the two skirts over the servant Cinderella's head. Staple the skirt around the waist.

4. Cut an apron from a fabric scrap and tie it around the waist of the skirt to cover the staples.

5. Turn the doll over to cover the servant doll and reveal Cinderella in her ball gown. Glue pretty trim on the gown to decorate it.

This flip doll lets you turn Cinderella's outfit from rags to a beautiful ball gown just like her fairy godmother did!

23

Little Red Riding Hood

tells of a little girl's encounter with a dangerous wolf as she goes through the forest to visit her sick grandmother.

Little Red Riding Hood Cup Puppet

Here is what you need:

two red cups and one blue cup of the same size

three paper fasteners

brown yarn

red ribbon

red nail polish

masking tape

scissors

white glue

Styrofoam ball that fits in your cup

pink poster paint and a paintbrush

Here is what you do:

1. To make the bottom of the cape, cut away about one third of one of the red cups, leaving the bottom of the cup intact. Turn the blue cup upside down for the dress and set the cut red cup over it for the bottom part of the cape. Poke a small hole through the bottom of the two cups.

2. Cut the top half off the second red cup. Line the inside of the cup with masking tape to create a surface glue will stick to. Turn the cup sideways to form a hood. Poke a hole through one side of the turned cup. Attach the turned cup to the body cups using a paper fastener pushed through the holes.

3. Paint the Styrofoam ball pink. Wrap a band of masking tape around the ball. Rub glue on the tape and glue the ball inside the hood for a head. Glue bits of yarn around the ball for hair. Push two paper fasteners into the head for eyes. Use nail polish to add pupils to the eyes, some rosy cheeks, and a little red mouth.

4. Tie a piece of ribbon in a bow around the neck of the puppet to make the tie of the hood.

Be very careful when taking your puppet for a walk in the woods!

"FEE FI FO FUM."

In **Jack** and the **Beanstalk**, a boy climbs up a beanstalk grown from magic beans and finds the castle of a giant.

Climbing Jack Puppet

Here is what you need:

- shoe box
- cardboard paper-towel tube
- green tissue paper in one or more shades
- fiberfill
- green, blue, and black poster paint and a paintbrush
- scissors
- markers
- yarn
- yellow, blue, brown, and red construction paper scraps
- masking tape
- white glue
- pipe cleaner
- four cardboard toilet-tissue tubes
- newspaper to work on

Here is what you do:

1. Stand the shoe box up on one of the short sides. The top side will hold the castle. Cut away one third of the top to make an opening for the beanstalk.

If this seems to weaken the box, you can put a strip of masking tape across one side of the cut to help the box hold its shape.

2. Paint the bottom inside of the box green for grass. Paint the rest of the inside of the box blue for the sky. Paint the long tube green for the beanstalk. Glue the green tube in the box with the opening of the tube under the opening cut at the top of the box.

3. Cut a hole through the box under the tube and slightly outside the area under the tube. Cut a piece of yarn more than twice as long as the tube. Drop one end of the yarn down through the top of the tube. Drop the other end outside the tube and down through the hole that is sticking out from under the tube. Tie the two ends of yarn together to make a loop of yarn that will slide up and down the tube when you pull it from underneath the box.

4. Fold a piece of yellow paper in half. Draw a 2-inch-tall (5-cm) Jack on the fold. Color the picture and cut it out. Color the other side of the picture. Glue the two sides of the picture around the yarn so that it will go up and down the beanstalk when you pull the yarn.

5. Cut a tiny house from paper scraps. Add details with a marker and glue the house in one corner of the bottom of the box.

6. Cut leaves from the green tissue paper to glue on the beanstalk.

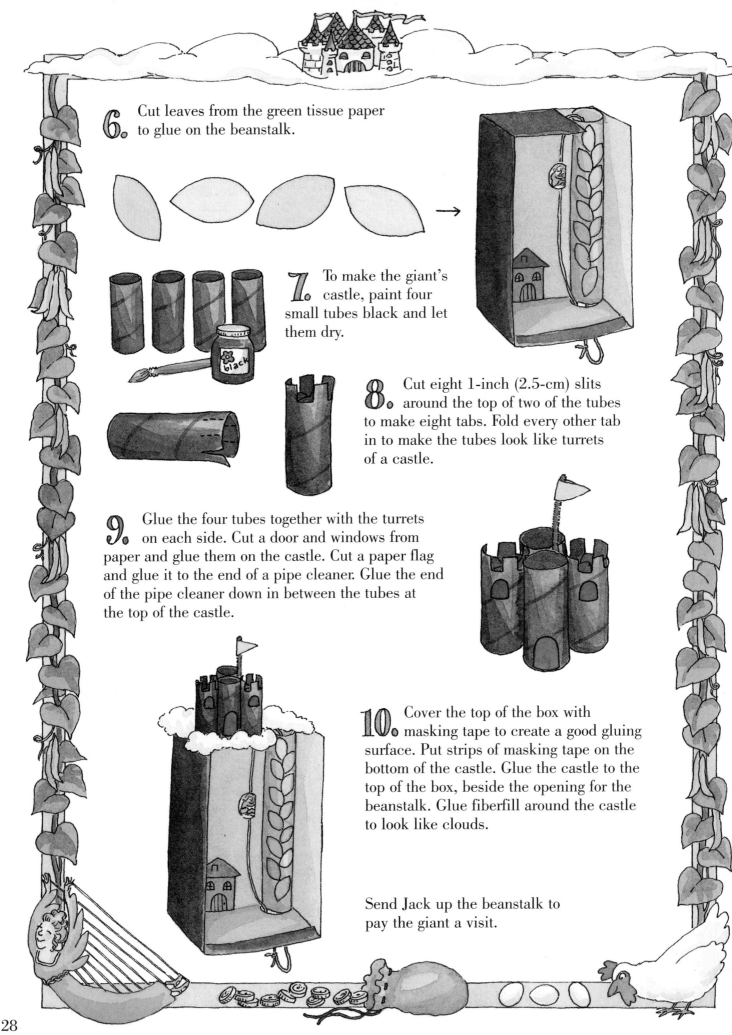

7. To make the giant's castle, paint four small tubes black and let them dry.

8. Cut eight 1-inch (2.5-cm) slits around the top of two of the tubes to make eight tabs. Fold every other tab in to make the tubes look like turrets of a castle.

9. Glue the four tubes together with the turrets on each side. Cut a door and windows from paper and glue them on the castle. Cut a paper flag and glue it to the end of a pipe cleaner. Glue the end of the pipe cleaner down in between the tubes at the top of the castle.

10. Cover the top of the box with masking tape to create a good gluing surface. Put strips of masking tape on the bottom of the castle. Glue the castle to the top of the box, beside the opening for the beanstalk. Glue fiberfill around the castle to look like clouds.

Send Jack up the beanstalk to pay the giant a visit.

In **Hansel and Gretel** two children lost in the woods come upon a gingerbread house beautifully decorated with candy.

Lunchbag Gingerbread House

Here is what you need:

- lunchbag
- scissors
- cellophane tape
- white glue
- red and brown construction paper
- four or more bottles of different-colored glues
- newspaper

Here is what you do:

1. Stuff the lunchbag about three-quarters full with crumpled newspaper. Fold over the top and tape it shut. This will be the house.

2. Cut a roof for the house from brown paper. Fold the paper in half and cut the roof out on the fold with half on each side of the paper. Glue the roof to the top of the bag with the fold forming the top of the roof.

3. Cut a chimney, door, and windows from the red paper. Glue the pieces in place.

4. Use the colored glue to decorate the gingerbread house with candies and squiggles of frosting.

This house looks good enough to eat!

In the story **The Golden Goose,** the poor boy wins the hand of the beautiful princess by making her laugh.

Sad Then Happy Princess

Here is what you need:

scissors

heavy 9-inch (23-cm) paper plate

white, red, and blue construction paper

black marker

paper fastener

aluminum foil

pink ribbon

yellow yarn

white glue

pink poster paint and a paintbrush

newspaper to work on

masking tape

Here is what you do:

1. Paint the bottom of the plate pink for a face. Let the paint dry.

2. Cut eyes from the white and blue paper. Glue the eyes on the face. Use the black marker to draw pupils on the eyes. Use the marker to draw a nose and eyelashes.

3. Cut a smile from the red paper. Attach the smile to the face with a paper fastener so that it can be turned upside down to make a frown.

4. Glue strands of yellow yarn around the face for hair. Make two long braids of yellow yarn to glue on each side if you wish. Tie pink ribbon around the bottom of each braid.

5. Fold a piece of aluminum foil in half, then fold it in half again so that the foil is four sheets thick. Cut a crown for the princess from the foil. Wrap the crown around the top of the head and tape the two ends in back of the plate using masking tape.

The boy with the golden goose turns this Princess's frown into a smile.

The Emperor's New Clothes

tells the story of a man whose foolish pride and vanity cause him to appear in public in his underwear!

File Folder Emperor

Here is what you need:

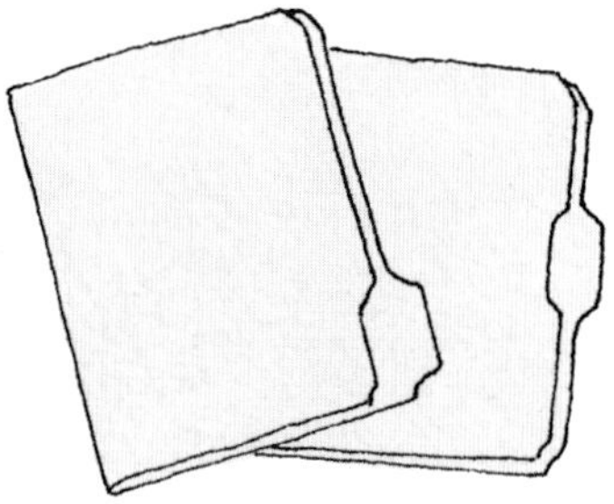

two file folders (you can use old ones)

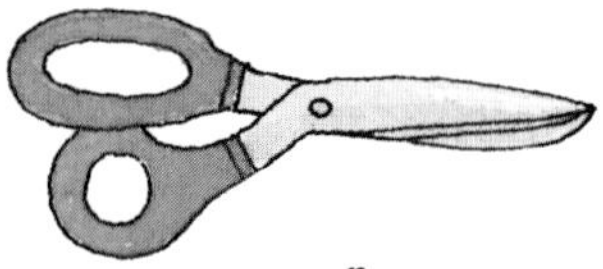

markers

scissors

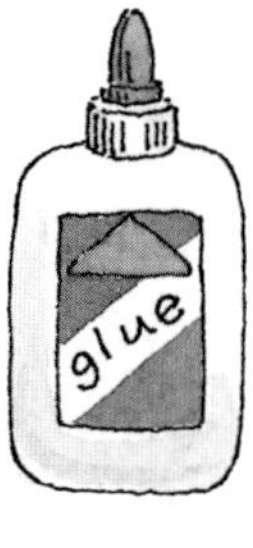

white glue

Here is what you do:

1. Draw the body of the emperor dressed in a fancy outfit on the front of one of the file folders.

2. Cut a head and feet for the emperor from the second file folder. Color fancy shoes on the feet. Color the face and hair of the emperor and a jeweled crown on the head.

3. Glue the bottom of the head to the back top of the folder so that it sticks out above the fancy outfit you drew. Glue the shoes to the bottom back of the folder so they stick out below the front of the folder. You now have an emperor dressed in his fancy clothes.

4. Open the folder up and draw the body portion of the same emperor wearing only his underwear.

How embarrassing!

33

In The Elves and the Shoemaker

two elves help a poor couple make beautiful shoes to sell.

Spool Elves

Here is what you need:

two large empty thread spools

four wiggle eyes

cotton balls

white glue

scissors

felt in two colors

red permanent marker

two 12-inch (30-cm) pipe cleaners

yarn

Here is what you do:

1. To make each elf, cut a piece of felt to cover the outside of a spool. Glue the ends of the felt together around the spool. The seam will be at the back of the elf.

2. Cut a pipe cleaner in half. String the two pieces through the center of the spool so that equal parts of the two pipe cleaners stick out of each end of the spool. Bend the ends of the pipe cleaners coming out of the bottom of the spool to make feet. Fold the top two ends down over each side of the spool and then bend the ends out to make arms.

3. Tie a piece of yarn around the middle of the spool to hold the arms down and make a belt for the elf.

4. Spread out a cotton ball and glue it over the top, sides, and back of the spool for hair.

5. Glue on two wiggle eyes. Draw a smile with the red marker.

You might want to display your two elves in an old shoe with sewing supplies such as a needle, thread spools, and small scissors. Elves like to keep busy!

The Ugly Duckling tells the

story of an awkward baby bird
that grows into a beautiful swan.

Swan Puppet

Here is what you need:

two 9-inch (23-cm) paper plates

white adult-size sock

black adult-size sock

white and orange construction paper

scissors

black marker

white craft feathers

stapler and staples

white glue

Here is what you do:

1. Fold two paper plates in half. Staple the edges of the two sides of the folded plates together. This will be the body of the swan.

2. Trace your hands on white paper. Cut the hand shapes out for wings. Glue a wing on each side of the plates. Glue some feathers on the wings.

3.

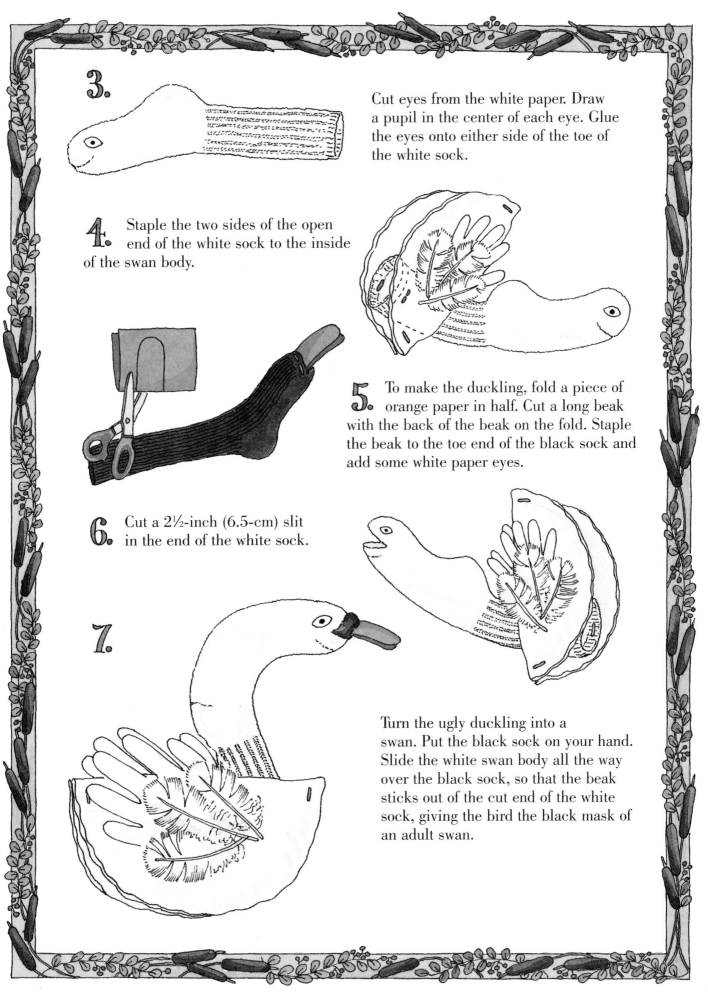

Cut eyes from the white paper. Draw a pupil in the center of each eye. Glue the eyes onto either side of the toe of the white sock.

4. Staple the two sides of the open end of the white sock to the inside of the swan body.

5. To make the duckling, fold a piece of orange paper in half. Cut a long beak with the back of the beak on the fold. Staple the beak to the toe end of the black sock and add some white paper eyes.

6. Cut a 2½-inch (6.5-cm) slit in the end of the white sock.

7.

Turn the ugly duckling into a swan. Put the black sock on your hand. Slide the white swan body all the way over the black sock, so that the beak sticks out of the cut end of the white sock, giving the bird the black mask of an adult swan.

In **The Fisherman and His Wife,** a man catches a magic fish that will give him three wishes if he agrees to let it go.

Magic Fish-in-the-Ocean Puppet

Here is what you need:

- shoe box lid
- blue poster paint and paintbrush
- small seashells
- green construction paper and bright-colored construction paper scraps
- clear bubble wrap
- thin string
- wide, clear packing tape
- gold glitter
- colorful pipe cleaner
- newspaper to work on
- hole punch
- scissors
- stapler and staples
- white glue

Here is what you do:

1. Cut a piece of string twice as long as the longest side of the box lid. Paint the string blue and paint the inside of the lid blue for the water and the sky.

2. Turn the lid so that it is as tall as it can be. Glue seashells along the bottom inside edge of the box to look like the ocean floor. Cut some seaweed from green paper and glue that along the bottom, too.

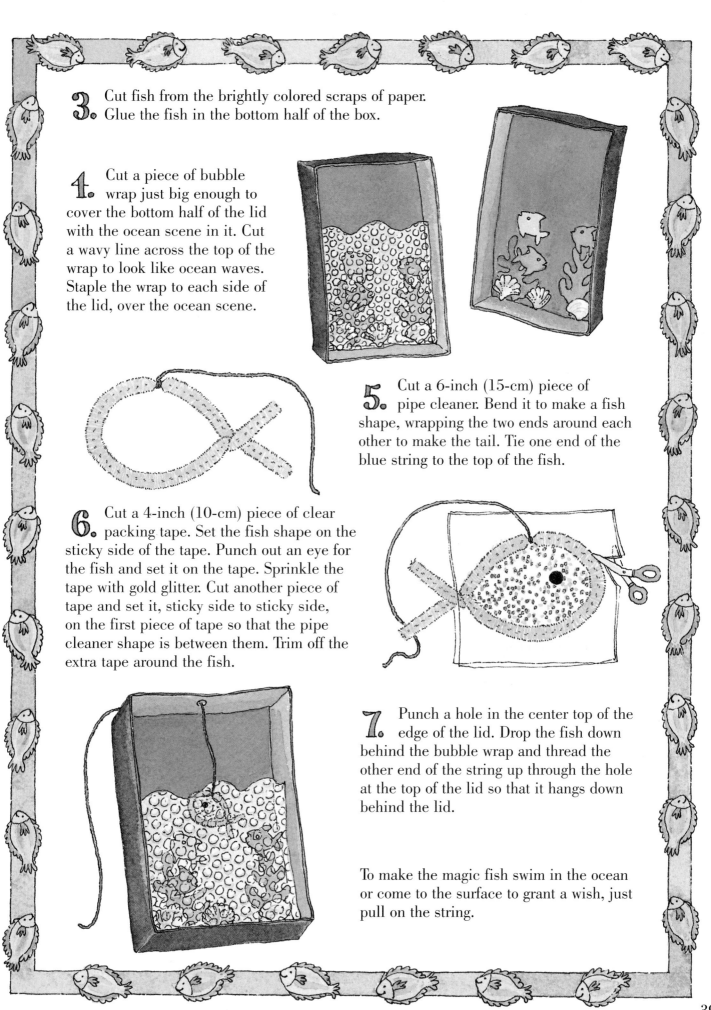

3. Cut fish from the brightly colored scraps of paper. Glue the fish in the bottom half of the box.

4. Cut a piece of bubble wrap just big enough to cover the bottom half of the lid with the ocean scene in it. Cut a wavy line across the top of the wrap to look like ocean waves. Staple the wrap to each side of the lid, over the ocean scene.

5. Cut a 6-inch (15-cm) piece of pipe cleaner. Bend it to make a fish shape, wrapping the two ends around each other to make the tail. Tie one end of the blue string to the top of the fish.

6. Cut a 4-inch (10-cm) piece of clear packing tape. Set the fish shape on the sticky side of the tape. Punch out an eye for the fish and set it on the tape. Sprinkle the tape with gold glitter. Cut another piece of tape and set it, sticky side to sticky side, on the first piece of tape so that the pipe cleaner shape is between them. Trim off the extra tape around the fish.

7. Punch a hole in the center top of the edge of the lid. Drop the fish down behind the bubble wrap and thread the other end of the string up through the hole at the top of the lid so that it hangs down behind the lid.

To make the magic fish swim in the ocean or come to the surface to grant a wish, just pull on the string.

In the story **Beauty and the Beast,** a beautiful young girl falls in love with a strange beast who turns out to be an enchanted prince.

Beast to Prince Doll

Here is what you need:

poster board

markers

paper fastener

scissors

Here is what you do:

1. Draw the head of the beast on poster board. Turn the head over and draw the neck and head of the prince attached to the beast head. Cut the two attached heads out.

2. Draw a body in fine clothing for the prince and the beast. Cut the body out. Use a paper fastener to attach the heads to the body so that one head shows above the shoulders and the other one is hidden behind the body.

3. Break the spell and change the beast back into the handsome prince!

4. You might want to make a beauty doll, too. You could make one face sad for when she thinks the beast is dying, and another face happy to use when she discovers he is the handsome prince.

The Frog Prince tells the story of a princess who did not want to keep her promise to a frog.

Frog Puppet

Here is what you need:

two 9-inch (23-cm) paper plates

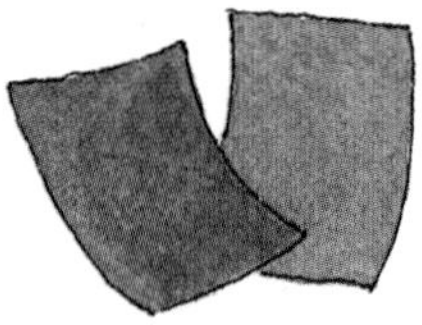

black and green construction paper

red and green poster paint and paintbrush

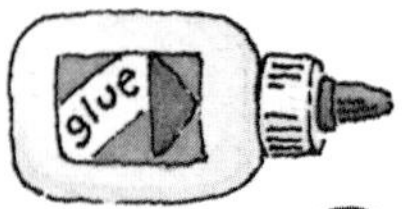

white glue

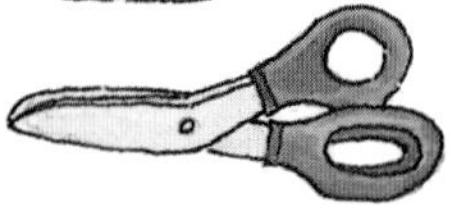

scissors

red party blower

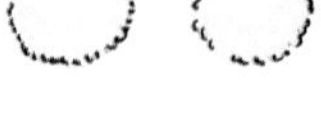

two large cotton balls

newspaper to work on

Here is what you do:

1. Paint the bottom of one plate green and the top of the other plate red and let them dry.

2. From the green paper, cut four frog legs about 5 inches (13 cm) long. Glue the bottom of the red plate to the top of the green plate. Fold the plates in half so that the red forms the mouth of the frog. Slide two frog legs in between the two plates on the bottom half of each side of the frog.

4 –

3.

Glue two cotton balls on the top green fold of the frog for eyes. Cut pupils from black paper and glue them on each cotton ball.

4. Cut a small slit in the center of the fold of the frog. Open the frog mouth and push the end of the party blower through the slit so that the mouthpiece sticks out in back of the frog and the curled part forms the tongue of the frog.

Surprise someone you know by blowing on the party blower to make the frog tongue pop out.

The story of **Rumpelstiltskin** tells of a little man with a very unusual name and the lady who had to guess it in order to keep her baby.

Story Box Theater

Here is what you need:

- small carton about 5 inches (13 cm) deep
- poster paint and a paintbrush
- white paper
- ribbon and trim
- markers or crayons
- two paper fasteners
- scissors
- thin cardboard
- old magazines and catalogs
- white glue
- newspaper to work on

Here is what you do:

1. Stand the carton on end so that the flaps open and shut like doors. Cut the other two flaps at the top and bottom off. Cut a 1-inch-wide (2.5-cm) slit down each side of the carton toward the back (which was the bottom) of the box.

2. Paint the entire box, inside and outside. Let the paint dry.

3. Push a paper fastener into the middle edge of each door. Tie a ribbon around one of the fasteners. To close the theater, just tie the ribbon to the other fastener to keep the flaps shut. Decorate the theater by gluing on the trims of your choice.

4. You will need to cut a sheet of thin cardboard for each scene you wish to include in the telling of the story.

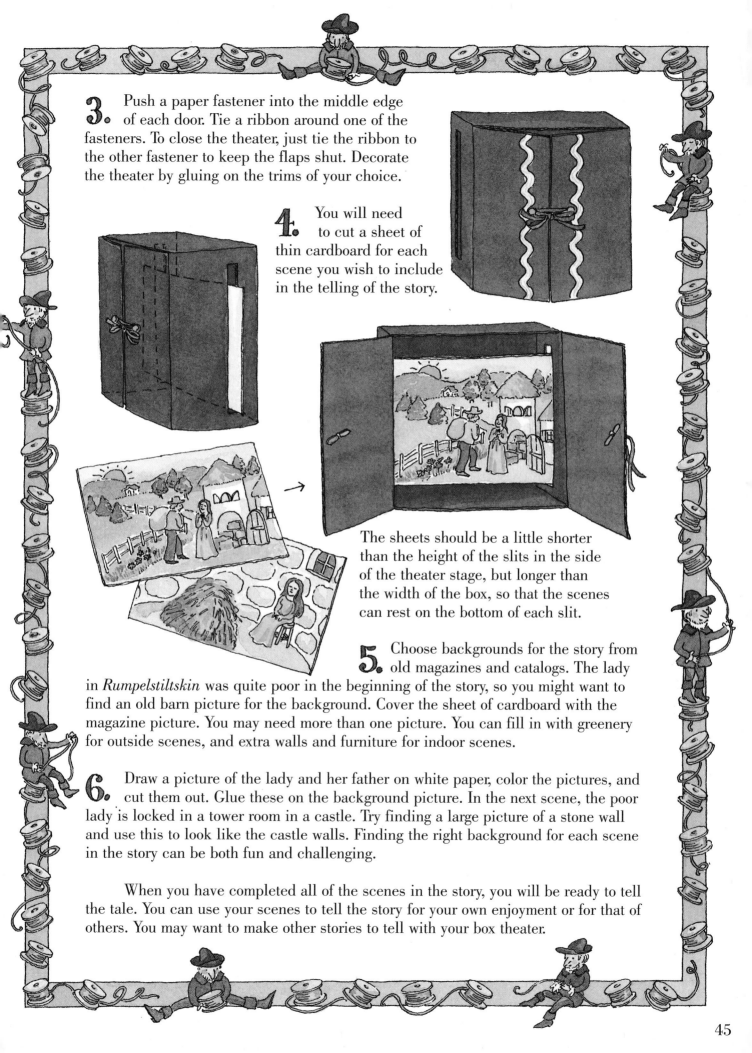

The sheets should be a little shorter than the height of the slits in the side of the theater stage, but longer than the width of the box, so that the scenes can rest on the bottom of each slit.

5. Choose backgrounds for the story from old magazines and catalogs. The lady in *Rumpelstiltskin* was quite poor in the beginning of the story, so you might want to find an old barn picture for the background. Cover the sheet of cardboard with the magazine picture. You may need more than one picture. You can fill in with greenery for outside scenes, and extra walls and furniture for indoor scenes.

6. Draw a picture of the lady and her father on white paper, color the pictures, and cut them out. Glue these on the background picture. In the next scene, the poor lady is locked in a tower room in a castle. Try finding a large picture of a stone wall and use this to look like the castle walls. Finding the right background for each scene in the story can be both fun and challenging.

When you have completed all of the scenes in the story, you will be ready to tell the tale. You can use your scenes to tell the story for your own enjoyment or for that of others. You may want to make other stories to tell with your box theater.

The princess in **Sleeping Beauty** was awakened by a kiss.

Wake Up Puppet

Here is what you need:

round salt carton with pour spout

masking tape

print fabric or paper napkin

pink, white, and red construction paper scraps

rubber band

blue marker

pink poster paint and paintbrush

scissors

white glue

brown yarn

Here is what you do:

1. Cut the bottom out of the salt carton. Cover the entire spout with masking tape. The outside needs to be covered so that the glue will stick to it. The inside edges need to be covered because they can be sharp. Do this carefully.

2. Paint the top of the carton pink for the face.

3. Cut eyes, a nose, and a mouth from construction paper. Color in the center of each eye with the marker. Glue the facial features on, with the eyes on each side and just below the spout.

back of eyelids

glue

4. Cut two eyelids, attached to each other, that are large enough to cover the eyes when set on top of them. Cut yarn eyelashes to glue along the bottom of each lid. Glue the lids to the spout of the salt carton. When you put your hand inside the carton, you should be able to open and shut the eyes by pushing and pulling on the spout.

5. Cut yarn hair to glue around the face of the puppet.

6. Dress the puppet by wrapping the salt carton in a pretty napkin and holding it in place with a rubber band. You can hide the rubber band by folding the napkin down over it.

Find a handsome prince to wake this puppet up with a kiss!

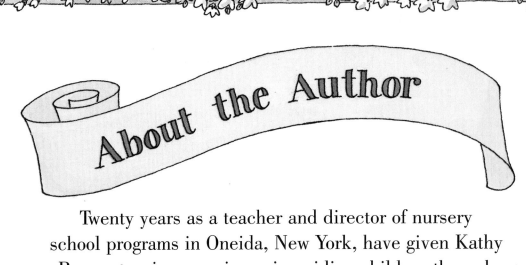

About the Author

Twenty years as a teacher and director of nursery school programs in Oneida, New York, have given Kathy Ross extensive experience in guiding children through craft projects. A collector of teddy bears and paper dolls, her craft projects have frequently appeared in *Highlights* magazine. She is the author of Millbrook Press's Holiday Crafts for Kids series, including *Crafts for Halloween, Crafts for Christmas*, and *Every Day is Earth Day*. She is also the author of *Gifts to Make for Your Favorite Grownups, The Best Holiday Craft Book Ever*, and *Crafts for Kids Who Are Wild About Dinosaurs* and *Crafts for Kids Who Are Wild About Outer Space*.

About the Illustrator

A resident of Andover, Massachusetts, Vicky Enright studied editorial design/illustration at Syracuse University. To date, she has utilized her talents as a calligrapher, a wallpaper designer, and a greeting card illustrator. *Crafts From Your Favorite Fairy Tales* is her first book.